D0672603

YOU DON'T HAVE TO BE A
WIMP
TO BE
ABUSED

An Easy Guide to Understanding
DOMESTIC VIOLENCE
AGAINST WOMEN

BEVERLY WALLIN

ST. JOHN THE BAPTIST PARISH LIBRARY
2920 NEW HIGHWAY 51
LAPLACE, LOUISIANA 70068

YOU DON'T HAVE TO BE A WIMP TO BE ABUSED
An Easy Guide to Understanding Domestic Violence Against Women

Copyright © 2016 Beverly Wallin.

All rights reserved. No part of this book may be used or reproduced by any means, graphic, electronic, or mechanical, including photocopying, recording, taping or by any information storage retrieval system without the written permission of the author except in the case of brief quotations embodied in critical articles and reviews.

iUniverse books may be ordered through booksellers or by contacting:

iUniverse
1663 Liberty Drive
Bloomington, IN 47403
www.iuniverse.com
1-800-Authors (1-800-288-4677)

Because of the dynamic nature of the Internet, any web addresses or links contained in this book may have changed since publication and may no longer be valid. The views expressed in this work are solely those of the author and do not necessarily reflect the views of the publisher, and the publisher hereby disclaims any responsibility for them.

Any people depicted in stock imagery provided by Thinkstock are models, and such images are being used for illustrative purposes only. Certain stock imagery © Thinkstock.

ISBN: 978-1-4917-9229-2 (sc)
ISBN: 978-1-4917-9230-8 (e)

Print information available on the last page.

iUniverse rev. date: 04/20/2016

ST. JOHN THE BAPTIST PARISH LIBRARY
2920 NEW HIGHWAY 51
LAPLACE, LOUISIANA 70068

CONTENTS

BE SET FREE

I am the rose my mommy gave me
Planted in a garden, complete with weeds.
The rose grew 'though choked by thorns and
Trapped by people pleasing, co-dependency.

Deep inside, the rose heard music resonating,
Chords that were off key and those with harmony.
She heard the difference between wrong and right.
And learned some new chords to make her garden bright.

The rose began to weed her garden seeking
To find the purity of her inner child, the rose.
The thorns no longer trapped her, she could clearly see;
'Though older and wiser, the original rose was finally set free.

~ Beverly Wallin and Josanne Franklen

FOREWORD

This book tells the story of a young girl named Jane. Through Jane, the reader gains invaluable insight into how little girls while still in childhood are socialized and in effect "brainwashed" to adopt the "Nice Girl Syndrome".

As a frontline worker in a Transition House for women and children and in my personal practice as a Dr. of Traditional Chinese Medicine, I have encountered these children. I have witnessed first hand the indoctrination of young girls coming from abusive homes and the effects of what the author refers to as "brainwashing." It follows them through their adult years, leading them into unhealthy relationships and setting them up to experience abuse as a normal state.

The reader learns about the art of detachment and other survival tactics. He or she ultimately walks through the cycle of abuse to learn how to recognize in a new and unique way the behaviors and language of abuse.

Ms. Wallin provides facts about domestic violence and offers tools, guidelines, and red flags to help identify and prevent abusive relationships. She sets out a quiz entitled

"Are you a good girl" which enables the reader to clearly identify risk areas.

This book is a must read for those individuals seeking to understand domestic violence and domestic abuse. The unique approach taken by the author enables the reader to self identify and understand the complex issues around domestic abuse. You will experience many "Ah Ha" moments.

- Dr. Bethany J. Hill, Dr. Traditional Chinese Medicine, Registered Herbalist & Acupuncturist, Social Activist for mental health reform, Former Director of the TCM Association of BC, Author: *Rhapsody in Thought* and *Food Cures for Common Ailments.*

Chapter 1

Introduction

"Courage doesn't always roar. Sometimes courage is the quiet voice at the end of the day saying, 'I will try again tomorrow.'" ~ Mary Anne Radmache

"I beg you take courage; the brave soul can mend even disaster." ~ Catherine the Great

Do you know what police officers consider to be one of their most dangerous encounters? It's entering into a scene of domestic violence. How many times do you think police are called in to do this? How often is the justice system involved in disputes, court hearings, and jail sentences related to domestic abuse? How common is this and who suffers? The answer is that it's extremely common and everyone suffers in some way. Our law enforcement, social workers, counselors, psychologists, and dentists suffer. The general medical, housing and social assistance programs will also save a lot of time, stress and money if this injustice is alleviated even a little. Not to mention the toll on our families and the awful legacy it leaves.

There is a shocking prevalence of domestic violence against women. Around the world one in three women experience domestic violence during her lifetime, with rates reaching 70 percent in some countries.[1] As many as 38% of murders against women are committed by their intimate partner.[2] More women aged 15-44 die, or become disabled due to domestic violence than the combined effects of cancer, malaria, traffic injuries and war.[6] This does not account for all the millions and billions of unreported cases of domestic abuse. Or, for the number of times a woman can be violated by different people in her lifetime.

I acknowledge that the statistics can also be skewed by "emotional vampires" claiming to be victims. There's a huge difference between "playing the victim" and being a real victim. A much larger majority of victims do not report the real thing.

Many women do NOT report Domestic Violence:

- For fear of retribution from their abusers and/or abuser's connections;

- For fear of not being believed;

- For fear of being ridiculed, rejected by friends and family, exposed and/or shamed;

- Because she is in denial or doesn't know she is being abused.

(This is especially true when the abuse experienced is not physically harmful in a noticeable way.)

The term "domestic violence" is often used only for physical abuse, while "domestic abuse" is used more often for emotional abuse. I will be using domestic violence and domestic abuse interchangeably since both are extremely detrimental to victims. If a victim is beaten physically she knows she is being abused, but without it she may not even realize that she is being violated.

In my opinion domestic violence can be extended to include childhood sexual abuse, rape, and any kind of abuse where someone or an institution has authority over someone else. It's not just restricted to family.

I use the terms "abuser" and "victim" loosely. Everything is not black and white, and people can be abusive to each other. The victim may also have some abusive behaviors. An abuser is not completely bad. An abusive man (or woman) may even start to recognize what he or she is doing, but has not yet learned how to change. The main difference is that an abuser has most, if not all, of the power and control in the relationship. Domestic abuse is about the power and control an abuser has over his or her victim(s).

Anyone can be a victim of Domestic Violence. Domestic abuse happens to people who are:

- Male, Female, or Transgendered

- Well-educated or Under-educated

- Young or Old

- Rich or Poor

- Gay or Straight

- Strong or Weak

And in:

- All Races,

- All Religions, and

- All Cultures of the World.

Domestic violence can also include any violence against an individual, especially when one is stronger or in authority over the other. Abuse can occur:

- On the jobsite,

- Between siblings and other children,

- At home,

- At school,

- In nursing homes, care homes and hospitals,

- Between friends and acquaintances,

- At any kind of organization,

- Between roommates, or

- Between trusted strangers.

Domestic violence can happen anywhere relationships happen. Domestic abuse can be:

- Financial - draining or controlling their victim's money, and/or spending family money and assets without the partner's consent;

- Spiritual - controlling or demeaning their victim's belief systems;

- Verbal – outbursts of anger, criticism or calling a victim names like stupid, lowering their self-esteem and causing fear;

- Emotional – causing their victims life to become stressed or restricted with the use of sarcasm, blaming, sabotage, passive aggression, down-playing accomplishments, and subterfuge;

- Psychological - playing head games to diminish, dominate and confuse a victim's sense of reality;

- Isolation – keeping victims away from family, friends or other support systems to have more power and control over them;

- Sexual - inappropriate sexual acts, sexually charged behaviors, refusal of intimacy or forced sex;

- Stalking - tracking their victim in any way, causing emotional upheaval, fear of safety, and stress;

- Threats - to harm children, other family members, pets or property keeping victims in a state of fear.

Abuse can be some, all, or more than the above. These different types of abuse usually overlap one another. For example, sexual abuse is definitely emotional, psychological and often physical abuse. Some writers simply call anything not physically harmful, as emotional abuse. Emotional abuse, however, is far from simple. It can mean anything from using guilt trips to ritual abuse, and even doing things that put others in physical danger, like driving too fast at the protest of the passenger(s.)

Most types of abuse leave no outward scars, but can damage a person deep within. A victim may think they are going crazy or that all the negative things their abuser says to them are true, including threats. Victims begin to question themselves and to believe they are unworthy of being treated better.

Domestic violence can be extremely subtle. So much so that even the victim does not realize that he or she is being abused. Domestic abuse is all around us, but it takes special eyes and ears to see it, hear it, and feel it. It is not something that we want to know about, but something that society needs to be informed about. Bringing consciousness to the horror of domestic violence is critical. Many victims' lives will be saved and also their quality of life improved if the public gets educated and involved.

As an advocate for all victims of abuse, my goal is to continue the journey of educating both men and women about the truth of this ever growing epidemic.

Through the fictional story of a courageous woman, Jane, you will get an inside view of:

- How and why many women find themselves in one abusive relationship after another;

- How devastating abuse can be to a woman throughout her lifetime;

- How difficult it is to get out of an abusive relationship and why, plus

- How to get healing and to learn some healing steps.

This book will be especially helpful for anyone, particularly a woman, who has been in an abusive situation, is in an abusive relationship currently, or who knows someone who is. Maybe you are wondering if you are being abused or are being abusive. It is helpful for everyone.

The first steps towards change are:

- Recognizing the signs, symptoms, and dynamics of domestic violence;

- Understanding how and why it happens;

- Recognizing abusers, abusive behavior and types of abuse;

- Prevention by learning how to help yourself and others;

- Providing safety for the victim; and

- Knowing where to get help and healing.

My hope is that we do not turn our backs on those who are in need of our help, including ourselves. With a little courage we can change ourselves and help the world to become a better place for all. Knowledge shines a light into the darkness and brings hope for the future.

- Beverly Wallin

Note/Disclaimer:

Jane is a composite character that has been put together from fiction and a variety of partially true stories. All names, places, and aspects have been changed to protect those individuals. As you read Jane's story you may wonder why the author doesn't mention how "Jane" could have received help. The fact is that she didn't think she needed help. Like most victims, Jane believed that she grew up in a healthy and happy home.

Even when she did seek help "Jane" would be too embarrassed to tell the truth. All the shame and blame are taken on by victims from what their abusers do to them. They think it's all their fault. (See Chapter 9 to the end of the book for more self-help information and glossary of terms.)

The "Tools and Guidelines," are not 100% accurate. They are not meant to be facts used to accuse or blame others. They are intended to help the reader to better understand domestic violence.

Chapter 2

Jane's Childhood

"The family unit plays a critical role in our society and in the training of the generation to come." ~ Sandra Day O'Connor

"Defense mechanisms locked me up into a prison of my own making." ~ Jane

Jane absolutely adores her tall handsome father with blonde hair and blue eyes. He is her hero. More than anything else, she desires to please him and to gain his unconditional love. But nothing she ever accomplishes seems to be good enough.

No one suspects that her father is an emotional manipulator. He can be very sociable and charming. He has a sharp wit and is often sarcastic, controlling and critical. Jane has no idea that his behavior is abusive.

Her father and mother never argue, but they both expect Jane to speak only when spoken to. Jane is not allowed to interrupt conversations or to express any opinions of her own. Her voice is stifled, just like many other children who grow up in abusive homes.

"If you don't have anything nice to say, then say nothing," Jane's mom and dad harp at her continually.

Jane believes that parents are all like this. This is Jane's "normal." She also perceives herself as lucky. Usually, all it takes is "the look." The look of disappointment on her father's face that controls her behavior more than anything.

My father doesn't discipline me with spankings.

There are no observable violent incidents, but this family is not healthy. The tension vibrates, and it is palpable. It seeps into Jane's subconscious mind, just like everything does for a young child, especially before the age of five. Because Jane is intuitive and intelligent she behaves in a winning fashion to gain her parents' love and attention. However, she is being groomed to become a co-dependent people pleaser and/or victim of abuse in the future. There is often a misconception that domestic violence means people are being beaten black and blue.

Emotional abuse is subtle, far beyond what a child could possibly understand. Sarcasm goes right over their head while touching their very soul/ subconscious mind. It sneaks in like a thief in the night.

Jane is brainwashed to "be nice." [4] Her parents are both more concerned about what people think of them as a family than they are about demonstrating authenticity. Jane struggles between being true to herself and pretending to be someone her parents and teachers want her to be.

She must tell the truth, whatever her parents decide is the truth. The standard punishment for "lies" is to be sent to her room until she comes out, apologizes, and admits the "truth." Normally, Jane just stays in her room and plays; she refuses to admit to something she didn't do. She is a strong-willed child and no wimp.

Jane talks to her doll, "I'm sure I didn't lie. What do you think Sally?"

"No," Sally agrees, "but maybe you can just tell them what they want to hear. Then you can do whatever you want. They don't have to know."

"But then I really would be lying, wouldn't I?" Jane is puzzled.

"You're being blamed for lying anyway. Don't you want to please your mom and dad, especially your dad?" Sally suggests, tempting Jane.

One-day Jane decides, *I'll tell Mom and Dad what they want to hear, period. Then I can do whatever I want.* Jane's intelligence and dramatic flair enable her to put on a good "act." Jane practices lying and discovers that it is definitely beneficial. The more she uses it the better she becomes. Jane discovers that telling half-truths work even better.

Lying is just one of the many "defense mechanisms" that Jane invents. This, and other defensive actions become habits that will be hard to change later in life.

Jane's father controls her co-dependent mother with criticism, sarcasm, and financial frugality. He controls

Jane in the same harsh manner, failing to understand his daughter and her emotional needs. Jane's mother isn't much better in that department. Mom remains very proper and distant with Jane and is stingy with her praise, especially under the watchful eye of her husband.

When Dad is out of town, her mom is much easier on her. Jane even confides in her mother about things she doesn't want her father to know about, like her boyfriends. One day, Jane tells her mom how wonderful it feels when a boy kisses her. Her first kiss by her first love.

Jane sighs. "My boyfriend, Ronny kissed me today. It felt wonderful! Is it okay for him to put his tongue in my mouth, and for me to kiss him back that way?"

Mom is vague. "What do you think?" This is a typical answer to a serious question, or, "You'll learn when you get older."

"I love him Mom. Ronny says he loves me too." Jane shares dreamily. "Come on Mom. I really want your opinion on this."

Mother looks concerned. "It's a hard question to answer. If you're serious with Ronny it could lead to getting pregnant, and I don't think you're ready for that yet Jane. You're only 16."

"How do girls get pregnant Mom? By kissing?" Jane thinks back to a movie; *a man and woman are kissing passionately, and in the next scene the woman is pregnant.*

Mom explains, "No, it doesn't happen like that, but one thing can lead to another. Just don't be alone with him and you'll be okay."

"What can French kissing lead to Mom?" Jane questions seriously.

"You'll find out when you get married. You're too young to know these things now," her mother hedges.

"Is there any way to prevent myself from getting pregnant?" Jane wonders aloud.

"Nothing is foolproof. Anyway, you are not old enough to be having this type of relationship It's best to keep yourself pure until marriage." Mother warns her daughter sternly, but fails to explain the reason it's so important.

One day, Jane uncovers the fact that Mother almost always spills the beans to Dad, who then criticizes and embarrasses her. She feels betrayed by her mother. Jane decides that no one can be trusted completely, especially females and authority figures.

She realizes that it is better to keep her secret thoughts to herself, and to make her own decisions. Jane copes very well, at least on the outside. On the inside, she is full of fear and is screaming with frustration.

Jane's parents do not allow Jane to take sex education at school; they put blocks on her computer, and don't allow books about sex in their home. Jane, of course, talks to her friends, but doesn't always get the right information.

Jane's parents are against abortion, no matter what the circumstances, and Jane knows that if she gets pregnant it will humiliate the family. She understands that she will never get any help from them, and probably be disowned.

It doesn't take long for Jane to understand what sexual intercourse is. She and Ronny are very close to it and she is beginning to want it to happen. Not knowing how to avoid pregnancy however, Jane thinks, *I don't want him to talk me out of breaking up with him; I don't trust myself.* Jane isn't concerned about remaining pure; she is concerned about ruining her life. *Being a virgin will insure I don't get pregnant.*

Impulsively, she lies to him saying, "I don't love you anymore."

She really does love him, or so she thinks. Jane doesn't understand until decades later, that real love is a choice. Jane lets fear motivate her. She isn't mature enough to make that choice at 16. Her mother is right, but Jane doesn't understand why.

This confusion will negatively affect her future relationships. Although inwardly rebellious, Jane is a co-dependent and easily attracted to narcissistic manipulators.

(See Self Theory in Glossary of Terms)

****

Four years earlier Jane enters junior high school. Jane's male teacher, Mr. Hanson, is very sarcastic, just like her dad. He has overly high expectations of his students. Wanting to please her teacher and to avoid criticism, Jane works especially hard. Her schoolmates are also driven to perfection. If they make a mistake or don't know the answer to a question, their abusive teacher humiliates them. The abuse at school reinforces the type of abuse she suffers from her father. Two of her male role models expect high performance, while neglecting the mentoring, character development, and emotional understanding that children and teenagers need for healthy self-esteem.

Children need physical contact too. Jane's father is stand-offish when she is a teenager.

One day, Jane feels so embarrassed from Mr. Hanson's teasing that she runs out of the class in tears. Mr. Hanson follows her to the girls' washroom. He's curious to know what the matter is. Jane is scared out of her wits but he seems genuinely concerned about her and surprisingly nice. He empathizes with her situation. Jane starts to like him.

The next year Mr. Hanson treats Jane much better. She continues to work hard and is his best student. He starts to give her special privileges, like chatting with her after class. Jane starts to trust him and thinks; *he really wants to help me with my troubles at home.*

One day Mr. Hanson invites her to come with him for a drive after school. He has something special to give her. It's a locket with his picture on one side. He instructs her to put her picture on the other side, to wear it under her clothes, and not to show it to her parents, or tell anyone where she got it.

Jane feels really special and believes that he loves and cares for her. She has had a secret crush on him ever since the last school year. *He really reminds me of Dad, but he is much nice*r. In actuality, Mr. Hanson is grooming her for sexual abuse. By fulfilling most of her emotional needs, getting her alone with him, and flirting with her, he is actually using Jane. Jane doesn't realize what is happening and doesn't share this experience with anyone. It's a secret between the two of them.

This relationship continues most of the school year. Jane begins to feel like his girlfriend but really wants to start dating some boys her own age. When she starts going out with a boy fairly regularly, Mr. Hanson becomes jealous.

"I'm very disappointed in you Jane. We can't be friends any more, if you have boyfriends," he insists.

She knows deep down that this connection with an older man is wrong. Jane talks to her new boyfriend about it and he tells her to stop seeing him.

"Why would you want to hang out with an old man?"

The next time Mr. Hanson suggests they meet, Jane sighs, "I can't see you any longer. I'm sorry, but my boyfriend doesn't like it and I don't believe it's right either." He has no choice but to accept it, however he gives her the cold shoulder after that, and she is clearly not his favorite anymore. Nothing is ever said. Jane carries on with her life pretending it never happened, but it does affect her.

A child under the age of 18 doesn't even have to be touched for some actions to be considered childhood sexual abuse, especially if the perpetrator has authority over them. Words, feelings and gestures can be used inappropriately.

Mr. Hanson treats Jane like he would a girlfriend, flirting and giving gifts to her. He is manipulating his young admirer for his own emotional desires. This is childhood sexual abuse. Jane is lucky to get out before something more serious occurs. Much later in her life, Jane realizes that Mr. Hanson could have lost his job.[3]

Since Jane is a co-dependent high achiever and Mr. Hanson a narcissistic perfectionist, it is a mutual attraction. Jane later realizes that she was too open with him. She learns that being open and honest; sharing her thoughts and feelings, are important in healthy relationships, but dangerous in unhealthy ones. She also feels shame for letting herself get involved, and blames herself for ending it so abruptly. Because Mr. Hanson acts coldly towards her afterward, her self-esteem drops several notches.[12]

Whenever she feels unworthy, Jane reminds herself of all the things at which she excels, with the subconscious desire of being "good enough." This boosts her self-esteem and increases her desire to do even better. But it is never good enough.

Deep down Jane wants to be loved just the way she is, and not for what she is able to achieve. She longs for her parents to listen to her, to understand her and to help her. Jane yearns for unconditional love.

When Jane tries to talk to Dad about anything resembling problems, or when Jane gets emotional, he harshly says, "Crying won't get you what you want."

Her father implies that she is trying to manipulate him by saying things like, "Don't think you can fool me with your sob story!" He is "projecting" his own manipulative behaviors onto Jane.

The truth is that Jane really feels upset; she needs to be heard and understood. Being accused of having ulterior motives, hurts her even more. Jane begins to believe that her feelings are "wrong" or "bad." She stops trying to share them.

Jane can no longer be authentic. Instead she lies to herself. She only expresses what she thinks other people want to hear. This leads to low self-esteem and feelings of being loved conditionally. Eventually Jane loses touch with her real feelings and her true self.

A healthy young person who is loved unconditionally learns how to show her feelings appropriately and knows that they are valid. Jane doesn't know how to express her feelings in a calm and assertive manner. All she knows is that whenever she attempts an explanation or desire at home, it ends up in an argument which can never be won. Most of the time Jane believes that she needs to yell if she is to be heard at all. Jane's parents make sure she understands that expressing herself this way is punishable. There seems to be no middle ground. Even if Jane is assertive her father misinterprets her message as aggressive anyway, like most abusers do.

Jane's father is aggressive. That's what Jane learns from him. She is either aggressive herself, or acts "nice" while actually displaying some symptoms of passive aggression like her father.

Jane often lies to her parents to get her own way. Or she "forgets" things, on purpose. Sometimes, she even takes a small amount of money from Mother's wallet, when angry.

Jane believes that she is growing up in a healthy and happy home. For her, this is normal. She has no idea that she is being abused. If anything, Jane thinks that she is the one who is defective.

"The basic difference between being assertive and being aggressive is how our words and behavior affect the rights and wellbeing of others."

~ Sharon Anthony Bower

It's likely that Jane suffers from: confusion, frustration, a sense of being violated, powerlessness, anger, anxiety, depression, worthlessness, defectiveness, shame, self blame, numbness, and loss of trust. Jane doesn't even know what her real feeling are. If there are places she can receive help, Jane doesn't think she needs it. Even if she does she is too ashamed to tell the truth.

If a parent, teacher or concerned adult sees a need in a child or teenager like Jane, they can direct him or her to a program like:

"Children Who Witness Violence."

These programs teach young victims to re-learn, how to get in touch with their feelings, and how to distinguish one feeling from another. They show victims how NOT to be re-victimized.

Local victim services, counseling centers and websites can help:

http://www.pssg.gov.bc.ca/victimservices/help/counselling.htm#children

CHAPTER 3

FROM INNOCENCE TO DISGRACE

"We're changing ourselves to fit the world instead of changing the world to fit women." ~ Gloria Steinem

"I would learn slowly that real girls aren't perfect and perfect girls aren't real." ~ Jane

Like most women Jane is socialized, or groomed, to act and to think the way she does. Jane develops some of the symptoms of a "Good Girl/People Pleaser" as described in *The Nice Girl Syndrome*. [4]

She is afraid of:

· Hurting someone's feelings

· Confrontation

· Rejection and abandonment

· Her own anger

· Becoming abusive or being called a bitch

· Looking too masculine

· Men not protecting and providing for her

Jane doesn't know that strong women can be kind and generous, while still taking care of themselves. She doesn't know that strong women have strong boundaries, demand respect, and realize that their voices have the power to change their world.[4] They are not "people pleasers." Strong women are authentic and assertive.

Jane is taught to be a "people pleaser." When she tries to be all things to all people, it is impossible to be her authentic self. Jane also allows others to take advantage of her gullibility. She never seems to learn her lesson and is often a victim of con artists. Jane has a huge investment in appearing to be nice, cooperative and charming, while inside feeling disagreeable, bored, or resentful. In my opinion, "being nice" is a set-up for becoming a co-dependent and/or victim.

Luckily Jane still has a strong will. She tries to please others, but not at the expense of her own happiness. She may cave into the demands of someone for a while, but she is no doormat either. This happens with one of her first boyfriends.

Jane meets him at a party where teenagers are pairing off and kissing each other. After a couple of dates, he asks her to go steady. She agrees only because he is pushing her and it seems like the popular thing to do. Jane doesn't know that an abusive person wants to get serious before his or her partner is ready. Her boyfriend keeps wanting to keep Jane to himself, exclusively. He always decides where they are going and what they are going to do. Jane begins to feel like she has to put on an act with him, to pretend she is attracted to him more than she is.

One evening, after their school's football game she decides that she's had enough of pretending and giving into his demands. They have a fight and Jane tells him that she wants to end their relationship. After months of caving in she finally sets a boundary.

This conflict escalates even more because Jane has taken off his school ring. Jane doesn't have it with her to return to him. Without giving her a chance to explain he tells her that she is using him, and that she made him fall in love with her just to get the ring.

Does this sound familiar? Do you think Jane's boyfriend is projecting his manipulative ways and/or narcissistic rage onto her?

He spreads this unfounded rumor around their school, warning Jane's potential future boyfriends, including Ronny. She feels hurt and misunderstood. This is a negative result of people pleasing, especially with an abusive person.

Jane begins to think that pretending to like someone maybe does make her a bad person. There are other times she breaks up with a boyfriend but some break up with her too.

Jane has a love-hunger from childhood from not getting enough unconditional parental love and acceptance, especially from her father. A father-daughter relationship is very important for relationships with other men. If Jane could experience healthy love and respect from her father, she will have healthier relationships.

Jane subconsciously longs to be loved just for herself, but she doesn't yet feel she is good enough. She is still trying to achieve some sort of perfection. This causes Jane to be vulnerable to abusive people.

***

Right after high school Jane enters the Physical Education program at her local university. She makes some new friends and hangs out with some of her old high school friends who also attend. Jane is still very naïve about sex. Her parents convince her that it is be best to remain a virgin until getting married. Jane isn't allowed to participate in Sex Ed; she's still ignorant about birth control, but knows that sex leads to pregnancy.

While trying out for the cheerleading team she meets Amy and, during the selection party, her new boyfriend, Steve, the football star. Steve informs her that he wants to start dating her exclusively. This was an obvious "red flag" that Jane misses. (See Tools and Guidelines.) She has a blind spot for abusers and once again judges poorly. She is vulnerable to all the attention from this popular boy. Steve makes her feel loveable and special. She still hasn't learned her lesson from past hurtful relationships.

Steve is in his second year of the Phys. Ed. program on a football scholarship. He starts dating Jane and spends time with her group of friends in the Student Lounge. Jane is in better physical shape than she has ever been before; she is tall for a woman and very strong physically.

Jane makes it very clear to Steve that she has a sexual boundary, no intercourse. She explains to him that she wants to remain pure for marriage. He seems to respect her for that. Jane only wants to keep her virginity so she won't get pregnant, but she keeps that to herself. They have a lot of fun together going to dances, parties and athletic endeavors like downhill skiing. Afterwards they make out, but Steve was pushing her to go a little further and further with him all the time. Still, Jane feels confident that Steve will keep his promise to honor her boundary, even after five months of dating.

They become close and Jane is really falling for him. One day they are at her parent's alone, laying on the living room floor. They start kissing and fondling as usual. But because they are still in their bathing suits it makes it easier for Steve to pull her bathing suit aside and also his own. While on top of her, he slips his penis into her vagina before Jane realizes what is happening. It doesn't hurt and he doesn't force her; but neither does he ask for consent, nor use a condom.

"No!" Jane cries out.

Steve stops immediately; she runs to the bathroom. Jane is horrified to discover that she has lost her virginity! At the same time, she is relieved that blood didn't get onto the carpet in her parents' living room. *What if they discovered it? What if she got pregnant?* Jane is more concerned about what her parents will think than anything else.

It never occurs to Jane that this experience is date rape. She believes it is her own fault for going too far with him.

27

The very next day Steve breaks up with her, just before her volley ball game, growling, "Grow up."

Jane is devastated and angry, but directs it into her ball game, trying very hard not to cry.

When her best friend, Amy, finds out about their break up, she reveals to Jane that Steve has been fooling around on her. Jane is surprised and hurt even more by this information, but somehow relieved. *At least I wasn't just one of his many conquests. I was special!*

"Steve broke up with me because I wouldn't put out," she tells Amy.

Amy looks stunned, "I thought you and Steve were doing it. He must have really liked you then."

This confirms Jane's idea of being "special," yet she knows she does not stay special.

Amy is concerned, "Are you okay? Did he hurt you?"

"He just hurt my feelings."

Jane thinks that Amy is a very religious person and against sex before marriage. She is too ashamed to tell her about the rape. Jane blames herself for letting it happen.

"He's a jerk. I know lots of respectful guys that would love to have you as their girlfriend," Amy encourages her.

Jane is happy that Amy respects and sees value in her, but inside she feels like damaged goods. She is confused, and wonders what she should have done to prevent this from happening. She keeps it all a secret, and holds her breath until her next period. Jane ponders Amy's comment that Steve must really like her, to go out with her without having sex. *Should I have let him have intercourse with me?* She wonders.

Jane doesn't blame Steve for doing what he did. She is hurt that he broke up with her and that he didn't really love and respect her the way she had hoped. *I didn't have a chance to explain myself and my fears.* In spite of Steve's treatment of her, Jane still thinks, *maybe the relationship could have been salvaged if I had been different, or better.*

Jane doesn't experience any physical pain in her experience with Steve. She simply has no experience and is afraid to get pregnant.

Jane feels the way most women do who are sexually abused; she feels ashamed and doesn't want anyone to know it happened. Her attacker blames her for the rape, and she believes that she is to blame for dressing too sexy or going too far.

Although things are improving, we know that many people still falsely believe that victims provoke the attacks of their abuser.

Some women who are raped or sexually abused become afraid to have another sexual relationship, even with someone they love and trust. This is usually the case with someone who is brutally raped by a stranger, but is originally quite normal. These women have no power and control over their situation, but they usually feel dirty and ashamed too.

Many others, like Jane, who are traumatized in a different way become promiscuous.

Jane "detaches" her real self from the experience of the rape and her consequent behaviors. This new defence mechanism, detachment is like watching someone else in a movie. It allows her to enjoy sexual experiences and to act out her subconscious anger against herself and others, while staying innocent and pure inside. Jane doesn't feel bad or guilty for her actions, but this keeps her from experiencing any real attachments to anyone, including herself.

Jane is setting herself up for more abusive relationships. The combination of taking on the shame for Steve raping her and feeling betrayed by him is just too much for her to handle emotionally. Detachment is a quick fix done on a subconscious level.

CHAPTER 4

LIVING THE DETACHED LIFESTYLE

"Our life always expresses the result of our dominant thoughts." ~ Soren Kierkegaard

"Detachment is not that you should own nothing but that nothing should own you." ~ Jane

Jane seems to be the same sweet girl as always. With all her physical strength and agility, no one thinks she's a wimp. She doesn't think she needs help either. Jane buries her angst deep inside, like other troubled youth who do not have the skills to express it. Instead, they do what's called "acting out." Troubled youth literally act out their feelings in wild, inappropriate or destructive behaviors. Jane is a "good girl" so can't do this directly. If Jane behaves badly she has no idea why she acts this way.

She has inadequate relationship skills and no one close enough to whom she can share her deepest feelings. Jane's friends and family are superficial. She keeps secrets from most of them, even Amy. *Adults and females in particular are not to be trusted.* Boyfriends her own age, on the other hand, are easier to trust. But they are not very good guides.

Now that Jane is no longer a virgin, and learns about several birth control measures; she goes on to have some sexual relationships, without setting her former boundary. Her thoughts and feelings lead her to act impulsively, without going through the process of healthy and careful decision making in choosing partners. Jane hypothesizes, *What's the point of abstaining from sex before marriage? I am no longer a virgin and I won't get pregnant*!

Just like that, Jane can do whatever she wants without facing the consequence of getting pregnant. She doesn't have to lie to her parents; she can act out instead. Jane begins to excuse her own rebellious actions by lying to herself.

Jane doesn't fall in love for a long time. She no longer believes that there is such thing as true romantic love. Subconsciously, Jane is afraid to become vulnerable again. Her relationships with guys become shallow and meaningless. She enjoys sex without getting emotionally attached.

****

In May, after her first year of university, Jane and Amy decide to go on a working vacation for the summer break. Jane has an old green Chevy, large enough to bring all their clothing and other necessary items. Like most young people they are confident that they are invincible. They head off to the ocean.

Getting a job in this busy Oceanside city is much harder than either of them have imagined. Away from her parents, Amy is also a changed person. She talks Jane into "go-go dancing" at a local club. It is scary at first but exciting.

Once Jane gets over the initial fear and embarrassment she begins to feel good about herself. It's a great job. She can enjoy dancing and drinking at night and still go to the beach during the daytime. Jane loves dancing and is getting really good at it. This is when and where she meets Dave.

She isn't attracted to him sexually at first; they are just good friends. They date for several months while Jane and her roommate are both having a great vacation, supporting themselves with a fun job. The beach and ocean are beautiful. Jane and Amy get great tans and flirt with the life guards. They visit all the tourist sights. Dave treats Jane to elegant places for dining and dancing. Life couldn't have been more perfect.

In the fall, Jane and Amy decide not to return to university for at least a year. Jane is given the opportunity to take a contract position posing topless for artists. She can do this during the daytime and still keep her nighttime job. Jane and Amy also do some lunchtime dancing at other clubs.

Jane finally lets Amy get to know her better, but she is the only one. Unfortunately, it back-fires on her.

Amy accuses Jane one day, "You're just using Dave, aren't you? He lets you drive his car and he takes you out to fancy restaurants. Why don't you tell him who you really are?"

Jane doesn't how to defend herself from such a degrading comment from her friend. Her first reaction is denial and shock. "What do you mean? I like him!"

"I know you're sleeping around; how come you're not sleeping with him?" Amy accuses her in a "holier than thou" manner.

Jane doesn't have an answer for this either. She stares at Amy, thinking. *What do you know about it anyway?* Yet, she wonders, *is Amy right?*

She is having a couple of casual sexual relationships with guys her own age. One's a life guard she met at the beach and the other's in acting school. Dave is ten years older than her, although he does look and act younger than his age. Jane thinks of Dave as an older brother or an uncle.

At 18, Jane isn't sexually attracted to older men. They represent authority figures, and Jane is afraid of them, except for Dave. She thinks she is able to twist him around her little finger. Jane doesn't know that he might continue to be in her life beyond her wonderful summer in the big city.

Jane becomes fearful of the lifestyle she is getting herself into, especially the after work parties at the clubs. Jane moves back home at Christmas but Amy returns without her. Jane looks for another job close to her parent's home.

While doing this, she becomes a victim of rape, again. This time it is by a stranger, who says he wants to pay her to take some semi-nude photos for his artist friend. Jane hopes the job will be similar to her previous one, and that she might get lots of work. Jane starts to get dressed after the photos are taken, but he grabs her from behind and tries to force himself on her.

"No! What are you doing? Stop!" Jane screams as he bends her over and pushes his erect penis into her vagina. With her athletic body, she manages to push her assailant away. There are negative consequences though. It doesn't take excessive violence to cause emotional and physical damage.

Jane feels so stupid and naïve for allowing herself to be talked into posing for a stranger. Once again she takes on all the blame and shame for the attack. *I should have known better than to be alone with him.*

He gives Jane gonorrhea and doesn't even pay her for the modeling session. *I'm glad no one was around to see me like that.*

She begins to worry about what her rapist might do with the pictures. In fact, her fear and thoughts of the rape just keep coming over and over. Jane is angry and ashamed, but holds it all inside, telling no one.

After this second rape, Jane becomes depressed and begins to have trouble sleeping. Sometimes she wakes up in the middle of the night, after having a nightmare. Rather than dealing with her problems however, Jane chooses to escape them. She deceives herself into thinking that she is just bored, and that the nightmares will go away.

Jane doesn't talk about any of this, especially to her parents. She is ashamed of what she "let" happen to her.

****

In March, Dave, comes to her hometown on his way to visit his family up north. Jane is ready for another adventure to escape her situation. She believes that running away from her problems will make her feel better. Impulsively, Jane decides to go with him. At least they wouldn't be having a sexual relationship. She wasn't ready for that after the rape. Jane is confident she can handle him.

However, like most victims Jane goes from one abusive relationship to another, seeking love and acceptance, believing that this time will be different. Since she is a co-dependent Jane can't help being attracted to a narcissistic individual. (See Self Theory in Glossary of Terms.) And because she is so hurt and vulnerable, she is easy pickings for an abuser. As a victim, Jane is also blind to the obvious "red flags." She is unable to tell the difference between safe and abusive men.

Jane is most likely a negative three co-dependent according to Dr. Rosenberg's "Self-Theory"[12], and is attracted to plus three narcissistic types in her intimate relationships. One of these narcissists will be her "Prince Charming."

According to Dr. Rosenberg, narcissism is in all types of the "Cluster B" Personality disorders (PDs,) which are related to abusive individuals. Even an undiagnosed narcissistic type can be abusive.

Antisocial, Narcissistic, & Borderline PDs are the most dangerous of the "Cluster B" PDs, and most likely to overlap one another. They fall into the plus four to five category. Their victims are extremely codependent, (negative four to five) according to Rosenberg's Self-Theory.

Many people have a mild narcissistic nature rated plus one or two, and can have healthy relationships with mild codependents. Personality Disorders are intense and must be diagnosed by professionals.

CHAPTER 5

ENGAGEMENT AND MARRIAGE

"When I eventually met Mr. Right I had no idea that his first name was Always." ~ Rita Rudner

"You learn more about a person at the end of a relationship than at the beginning." ~ Jane

Dave is crazy about Jane. He asks her to come with him to meet his parents and extended family. They live on a ranch with horses and cattle. To a city girl like Jane, this sounds like an exciting vacation. She already knows how to ride horses and loves it. Jane falls in love with his family and the outdoor lifestyle.

Jane is ecstatic to go on a cattle drive with Dave's family. They are moving the cattle to a nearby island to graze on the fresh grasses from early spring to late fall. When they arrive at the right spot the cattle are loaded onto a barge. It is a short trip. Jane and Dave enjoy several hours alone together as they wander around the island. He instructs her about farm life. Jane listens, fascinated.

This exciting period of time doesn't last long enough for Jane. It is just a holiday. Dave makes a plan for them. They move to the city for work. They share an apartment for the sake of convenience, but begin a sexual relationship anyway. A month later, Dave talks her into getting engaged. It is Jane's detached self that says, "Yes."

Immediately Dave takes control. He will not allow her to do the type of work she has done before, "go-go dancing" in front of other men, or posing for artists. Jane takes a job working in a restaurant, and hates it.

It doesn't take long until Dave has trouble getting steady contracts in the city. After less than a year together as an engaged couple, he drives hundreds of miles away where there is more work. Jane is left alone in their apartment with her absolutely horrendous job. She visits Dave's family at the ranch most weekends but is getting depressed. She blames Dave for her loneliness and sadness. Subconsciously Jane feels abandoned.

A couple of young guys live on the top floor of Jane's apartment. They love to party. When they keep asking her to join them, she finally gives in. They are into alcohol and drugs, like most young people are at parties; Jane takes part. Pretty soon it becomes a habit and she meets some interesting and attractive young men.

Jane decides that she wants Dave to stay away. *After all, we're just engaged, not married yet*. At 19 Jane isn't ready for such a serious relationship.

Jane informs Dave over the phone, "I want to break off our engagement, at least for now."

"Why, what's going on there?" he asks suspiciously.

"What are you implying? I just want to go home. I'm not happy here without you." Jane states more confidently than she feels.

"Wait for me first. I'm coming back." Dave insists.

He drives non-stop back to her, leaving his job temporarily. He convinces her to come with him to his new place of work that is across the country. Jane feels loved and special again. *He really does love me* she coos to herself. They load all their personal belongings into the car and drive for nearly one full day, stopping at OK Falls for a romantic engagement holiday.

This is another impulsive move by Jane. Both times she leaves her home to be with him they are always in a hurry. Dave has to be somewhere by a certain date. Jane doesn't realize that he is doing this on purpose. He is pushing her to make commitments before having time to really think about the consequences. Dave is taking control before Jane even notices. Again, she misses all the "red flags."

Jane assumes that Dave must be living in an apartment by now, since he's been working at his new job for several months. When they arrive at their final destination, Jane is disappointed that his accommodation is just a motel on the edge of town.

Jane thinks that Dave should have found them a nice place to live before having her join him. Instead, he leaves her in an isolated place. It is a totally new city for her and she doesn't know anyone. Since he is older, Jane is quite dependent on him, much like she would a father. Victims of childhood sexual abuse feel unable to care for themselves even in adulthood and Jane is a hopeless romantic.

"If a man expects his woman to be an angel in his life, he should first create a heaven for her." ~ Jane

Jane is not very happy alone all day with nothing to do. She gets bored one day. Jane impulsively takes the bus and walks to Dave's construction site. Jane is excited. She will surprise him and then get a ride home with him. Jane knows that if she calls first, he'll probably tell her not to come. When she arrives, Jane finds out that he has already left!

Jane doesn't have any more money for the bus ride back and can't remember the phone number for the motel! She asks at his workplace if someone can give her a ride back home, thinking it will be safe. *After all, they know Dave*, the contractor of the job.

A seemingly nice young man offers but, instead of taking her home, drives her out into the country, thinking he can take advantage of her. Jane soon sets him straight. He is surprised that she doesn't want to make out with him, and he becomes frustrated. Dave's cohort doesn't force Jane to do anything, but he is going to leave her out in the middle of nowhere.

Jane insists indignantly, "At the very least, you can drop me off at the outskirts of town."

When Jane finally gets home, Dave is irate. "Where have you been?"

After Jane explains, he demeans her. "How can you be so stupid?"

Dave blames Jane for the actions of another male. He is jealous, thinking that she is attracting the attention on purpose. Jane feels guilty for just being who she is. She doesn't think anything is strange in Dave's reaction; Jane is used to being treated this way. This is her "normal." A healthier man would have been outraged at the guy who had done this to her and would have told her that it wasn't her fault. Instead of being comforted, Jane is verbally abused.

The honeymoon stage is now over. The tension increases between Dave and Jane when Dave isolates and controls Jane. He does this by keeping her at their motel all day, not wanting her to talk to people without him there. When Jane doesn't do as she is told, the explosion comes in the form of verbal abuse.

An explosion doesn't have to be an act of physical violence. After the explosion it's back to the honeymoon stage of "affection," followed by tension and explosion again, going around continually in a cyclical fashion.

(See Chapter 9)

*****

Soon they get an apartment together and a puppy. The honeymoon stage of the cycle is on again. They call their dog Kalua, after the bottle of kalua that pays for her. She is their first "child."

Jane's parents think Dave and Jane should get married, since they are living together and already engaged. They offer to put on a wedding for them in Jane's old home town.

Since Dave doesn't have much money, he is happy to take them up on the offer. Jane isn't sure about getting married so soon. Dave manipulates her into believing that this is the perfect time. He doesn't tell her that it is because he has no contracts in the near future. He can rely on her parents for now. Jane is fooled into thinking; *Dave is always right. He's taking care of me.*

Jane's parents even pay for the flight to her hometown and pick them up at the airport. At her parent's home, however, they aren't allowed to sleep together. *How old-fashioned!* Jane sleeps in her old room and Dave on the sofa.

The day before the wedding Jane has a gut feeling that she is making a big mistake. *Do I even love Dave?* Jane makes up reasons in her head to go forward:

- *Dave really loves me and I really like him.*

- *I want to be married and have children.*

- *Dave's as good as the next guy.*

- *How would her parents feel if they spent all that time and money for nothing?*

- *What about the guests coming in from out-of-town?*

- *What about all the presents? They'd all have to be returned.*

Jane is concerned about these minor practicalities and doesn't see the big picture for what it really is. This is an important decision! But, Jane is a brainwashed, co-dependent people pleaser. She almost always puts others before herself and doesn't want to disappoint them, especially her father. She knows she will feel so guilty if she messes up all the plans everyone has made.

Jane has what is called, "The Cinderella Complex,"[13] meaning she fears her own independence; she wants to be taken care of. This is due to childhood sexual abuse and co-dependence. Since Dave is 29, Jane believes he will just automatically stop using drugs and alcohol, and change into a church-goer like Daddy. Jane thinks she can control him. She believes in the fairy tale, "…and they lived happily ever after."

Jane and Dave, like many young couples, have a lot of naive expectations of each other. They do not all include abusive behavior, however. It doesn't take long for Jane to discover that many of her expectations of love, care, and respect are not going to be met.

Jane and Dave settle into the domestic lifestyle. At first she enjoys making exquisite meals. When she asks Dave if he likes her cooking he usually dismisses it as just, "filling the hole." Over time it gets even worse. A typical conversation about her meals would go like this:

"What the hell is this crap?"

"I made it especially for you. I spent hours cooking," Jane replies in disappointment.

Then silence, followed by, "Get me a beer."

Dave sits down in the only comfortable chair in the living room and watches the hockey game. Jane sheds a few quiet tears in the kitchen while cleaning up. After a few times of trying to please Dave with nice suppers, she gives up and prepares what he really seems to want, meat and potatoes. And beer, of course.

On weekends, they usually go to a bar, and if Dave is drunk enough he dances with her. Or, they go to a house party and do the same thing. Drinking, dancing, and less than stimulating talk with his drunken friends. Dave completely controls their social life and does not want Jane to do anything on her own.

Like many victims Jane defends him. When he won't dance with her, Jane explains, "It just takes him a while to warm up before wanting to dance."

Jane doesn't even suspect that she is a victim. She believes their relationship is okay. Their life seems normal. They sometimes enjoy skiing together and playing cards on the weekends with Dave's friends and their wives. They get together for hockey and football playoff games or to go out dancing, which she especially enjoys. Jane is even used to Dave drinking too much and being unruly from time to time. Deep down, however she is not satisfied with this lifestyle or her marriage.

Jane needs more challenge. She tries a job at a grocery store and hates it, Jane starts taking some classes at the local university. She explains to Dave that if she gets her degree in Recreation she can make more money. She thinks to herself, *if I can get a job as a Recreation Counselor I will have some fun and be happier.* But, it isn't working.

Jane is experiencing emotional abuse, verbal abuse and isolation. She is unaware of the following "red flags." This relationship is moving forward at a rapid pace, starting with living together for convenience; a sexual relationship; engagement to be married; moving into a more permanent home with a dog; and marriage, all within one year. Common to abusers Dave pushes Jane into making these hasty commitments before she is comfortable.

Dave has this all planned from the beginning: romance her, get her away from her friends and family into an isolated situation, and make her dependant on him.

Jane and Dave go through "The Honeymoon Cycle of Abuse" many times. Jane feels abandoned and isolated. Dave is beginning to take all the power and control in their marriage. Since she is raised in an abusive family where her father is dominant and controlling, Jane misses Dave's strategies to increase his power and control. She doesn't see through the lies and the manipulation. Jane doesn't know that she is in an abusive marriage.

Dave often uses guilt to control Jane. It works because Jane wants to please him, just like she had her father. Dave says things like:

·   "You don't love me," when she is angry, sad, or just not in the mood for having sex with him.

- "You never buy anything special for me on my birthday," even though she has no money for things like that, because he controls the money.

- "Why don't you talk to our friends more often?" when he never makes an effort to talk to the few friends Jane has.

He also uses Jane's abandonment issues to his advantage:

- He never calls her if he will be late coming home, and then teases her for worrying.

- He hardly ever answers or returns her phone calls.

- He leaves her alone quite often for no reason at all.

Jane is trying to feel better by going to school part-time while taking care of their home, but still Jane isn't happy. She is alone.

CHAPTER 6

RAISING A FAMILY IN AN ABUSIVE HOME

"What lies behind you and what lies ahead of you pales in comparison to what lies inside you." ~ Ralph Waldo Emerson

"I feel like I'm trapped within a cage, although I'm free to leave. Only my feelings of fear and rage are holding me prisoner here." ~ Jane

Dave often goes to a bar with the guys after work. He never tells her where he is. One evening she calls a couple of places where she knows he hangs out. She hopes she can join him.

Dave comes to the phone in an angry mood and speaks harshly. "Don't ever call me here again; it embarrasses me in front of my friends."

When he arrives home that night Jane lies, "The reason I called was because I'm concerned about you. What if something happens to you?"

His only reaction, "Don't worry about me!"

In a healthy relationship this wouldn't happen, but Jane is used to having her feelings disregarded. It is partially true that she is concerned about him, but mainly she feels left out; Jane doesn't tell him that.

Why doesn't Jane tell him that she wants to be included? Does she think that he doesn't want her there? Is she afraid of being rejected? On a subconscious level the answer is a definite "Yes." Jane also wants to remain in "the honeymoon stage."

Jane allows Dave to control her; she knows he will never really abandon her. During the honeymoon stage of the cycle he professes his love frequently, showing it by taking her out to nice restaurants and buying her expensive jewelry.

Victims and abusers have intimacy and abandonment issues. They are afraid of getting too close to anyone, and revealing their inner selves, for fear of losing that person. *If she/he really knows who I am, she/he will hate me and leave me.* It becomes a dance of love, moving forward and backwards. If one partner gets too close, the other backs away. When one partner moves away, the other moves forward. This can also happen in healthier relationships, if both parties have been victims of domestic violence or have lost loved ones in childhood.

After the first year of marriage, Jane gives birth to a baby boy, Thomas. To a man like Dave, a son is proof of his manhood. He brags to his friends for a time but quickly loses interest. Before Thomas is even a one-year-old Dave works out of town again, for weeks at a time.

When September comes, Jane goes to school full-time and is kept busy raising a child, and taking care of their home all by herself. She starts to have trouble sleeping again; she becomes depressed and has panic attacks. Jane is stubborn and persistent, refusing to take medication. She keeps on pushing herself, like the perfectionist she is, managing to get through the school year without support. Jane doesn't have anyone close enough to whom she can share her deepest feelings. Even back home, all Jane's friends and family are superficial. The positive thing Jane learns is that she can survive by herself. In the spring Jane asks Dave to leave.

Dave threatens Jane. "No way. If you don't want to be with me, you leave. But you'll never get Thomas. He stays with me."

Jane believes Dave's threat; she remains with him. *I can never leave my child. Where would we go? How would we live?* Jane has no idea that she can get help. When Dave needs to move again to get work Jane goes with him.

Jane doesn't realize that abusers almost always refuse to leave the family home. They often want to keep the children to maintain control over their victim.

****

Two months later, Jane is pregnant again. The birth of their second child, Samuel, is the beginning of more severe abuse. Jane has to breastfeed Sammy since he is a colicky baby and allergic to regular milk. Dave ignores Sammy and says he is repulsed by Jane's breastfeeding. This is his excuse to stay out late, until the bar closes.

By the time Dave gets home, Jane is exhausted and not in the mood for sex. Dave, feeling entitled to use her body, forces himself on her. Jane also believes the lie that it is his "right" as a husband.

Even when Jane says, "No," Dave keeps her awake until she finally gives in.

This is sexual abuse, or marital rape.

"I only existed when he needed something from me." ~ Jane

Anger and bitterness begin to grow in Jane towards Dave. She doesn't know how to deal with these feelings. When they go to dance parties she "acts out" by flirting with other men. Dave gets jealous and slaps her in front of everyone. He blames Jane for his behavior. Jane leaves him for several days, staying with a girlfriend.

When she gets off work a couple of days later Dave follows her and begs her to come back home. He actually cries and promises to change. Another honeymoon cycle is complete. This isn't the first time, but he never hit her before. The abuse is escalating, and Jane is still taking the shame and blame onto herself. She even believes that she deserves the punishment because of her flirtations with other men. She enjoys dancing with them when Dave is unavailable.

Jane feels empty inside. *There must be more to life than this*, she sighs in desperation.

Jane starts to search the spiritual side of life and finds some fulfillment. Unfortunately, this only causes more abuse. Dave refuses to let Jane go to Women's Retreats or to let her take their children to church. He slams her religious books closed when she is reading. He turns off TV or radio channels that she is watching or listening to. Dave makes fun of her beliefs in front of Tommy and Sammy.

"Mom believes in Satan." He taunts her like a juvenile boy.

This is religious abuse: making fun of, belittling, or refusing to allow a partner their beliefs.

When he is out of town, Jane is free to do as she pleases, within limits.

She doesn't have access to much money. Dave makes a good living now, but spends most of it on himself. Jane has to pay all their necessary bills. There never seems to be any money left over at month's end. In fact, they are getting into debt. They pay off their debts by re-financing their mortgage on the house. Even when Jane begs him to stop spending so much money, he does not heed her advice.

This is called financial abuse. Healthy partners agree on how family money is spent.

Jane is making some girlfriends of her own; it usually takes her a long time to find someone with a similar personality and intelligence. Finally, she meets Diane, who becomes her best friend. Diane has a daughter the same age as Sammy and they both like to be active. They go on canoe trips in the summer and cross-country skiing in the winter. Jane really enjoys being able to share her feelings and to trust someone.

One day, after Jane shares some of her marital problems with Diane, her friend explains, "What you are experiencing Jane, is domestic abuse." She goes on to answer all of Jane's questions the best she can.

Diane talks Jane into calling a transition home for women and children fleeing abuse. The worker who answers the phone seems very friendly. She assures Jane that her children and herself will have their own room and will be safe with them. Jane answers all the questions required and is invited to come as soon as it was safe to do so.

Chapter 7

The Transition Home

"Change your life today. Don't gamble on the future, act now, without delay." ~ Simone de Beauvoir

"I thought I was finally safe but realized that I still had to protect myself and my children." ~ Jane

Jane and her two children pack up and leave home while Dave is out of town. She writes a letter and places it on their bed, along with several tears.

"I am leaving you for good this time. The children and I have a safe place to stay. I have no intention of calling you. Please do not try to contact me or to find me. You will be hearing from my lawyer when the time is right."

Jane feels bad about taking the boys away from their daddy, but the workers at the Transition House explain how important it is for her to do so. It's something to do with legalities. She has a much greater chance to keep them the majority of the time if she has them with her. This will also help her to find subsidized housing and get larger welfare checks for her transition period.

Jane arrives at the shelter a couple of weeks before Christmas. The staff are very busy collecting hampers for former residents in need, and in planning the resident and ex-resident Christmas Party. While this is happening, some residents who normally would never have been permitted to stay, are there anyway.

One gal is drinking alcohol and doing drugs. Another resident has a mood disorder and is in the manic stage. One hid when things got too crazy. Jane tries to help her, but this woman trusts no one. She suffers from a lifetime of severe physical and emotional abuse, and suffers from post-traumatic stress disorder (PTSD). Jane learns that panic attacks, depression, anxiety, mood disorders, and substance abuse are common side effects from living with an abuser.

There are a couple of families with whom Jane and the children can relate. They share their stories, and Jane feels like she isn't so alone after all. The Transition House holds weekly group counseling meetings which help Jane to understand abusive relationships. The Child Support Worker has counseling for the children, and tips for parenting through these difficult times.

After the maximum 30-day stay at the crisis transition home, Jane and her boys go to a second stage transition home. They have their own apartment; it is much more comfortable. They still have the help of staff from the first stage Transition Home but also their privacy. She attends a program for recovery from abuse, and her children have their own program. By the end of the year they are ready to move on with their life, or so they think.

Dave is very abusive during the divorce proceedings and the separation of assets. He is trying to get sole custody of his oldest son, Tommy, however the court decides that it would best to keep the children together with Mom. Dave is awarded visitation rights for both children, which means taking Tommy and Sammy most weekends. Both parents are equally responsible for making the major decisions in their children's lives. Dave is ordered to support Jane and the boys financially, although he hardly ever makes the payments, willingly.

It takes nearly 18 months to officially complete the settlement. Dave is angry at both her and his lawyer when he learns that he has to pay even more spousal and child support.

Dave continues to create havoc in Jane's world for a few more years. Jane still isn't free.

Abusers will use anyone and anything, including their own children to maintain control over their victim. Dave gives her a hard time about what the children are wearing or how they are looking. Dave is a "Disneyland Dad," giving gifts and taking them out to fun places. He picks them up late and brings them back too early or too late. Jane isn't able to count on him; much like before they split up.

Jane, Thomas, and Samuel slowly learn to deal with abusive people. Jane cuts off contact with Dave, and so do the children when they are old enough to make their own decisions. This threesome is much better prepared to carry on with a normal life.

Jane identifies with the quote:

"It took me quite a long time to develop a voice, and now that I have it, I am not going to be silent." - Madeleine Albright

CHAPTER 8

HOW JANE HEALED FROM HER ABUSIVE RELATIONSHIPS

"Find a place inside where there's joy, and the joy will burn out the pain." ~ Joseph Campbell

"One day I'll be free from the chains that hold me. I'll soar like an eagle and leave my cares behind me. ~ Jane

Jane wonders why she's not a lot happier now. The truth is she often longs for the life Dave and she had together as a family - the good things like family activities, holidays and other family outings. She feels guilty for being the one to break up the family and misses the sense of belonging. His friends blame her for the separation.

Jane is suffering from what is known as, *Complicated Grief*. This type of grief is often worse than the loss of a loved one through death.

Why am I grieving something that was so horrible? Jane is dismayed and confused.

What she is really grieving is the life she always thought would be hers. Much of Jane's life has been wasted, dreaming of, and working for something that wasn't going to happen.

Why and how did this happen?

Ideas from books, including Alice Miller's The *Truth Will Set You Free*[5] help Jane to understand why she is drawn to abusive people. This helps her to forgive herself and to begin to heal. Miller focuses on childhoods that include spanking and humiliation. She says that this "causes a type of blindness in adulthood that can lead to being manipulated..."[6] Adult children have not developed the ability to see through lies. This is the kind of parenting and education that Jane received. The major authority figures in her life try to break her will in order to make her obedient. This leaves long-lasting imprints on the way she thinks and relates to others as an adult.

Instead of giving in, Jane learns how to hide her natural feelings, rather than change them to suit others. Jane is a strong-willed child, and that child is still a part of her. She is a habitual liar, pretends to feel and to act the way she thinks she should, to avoid punishment. She can not properly process what is going on, because she usually doesn't know why she is being punished.

As a teenager and a young adult, Jane often puts on a rebellious attitude, *I don't care what other people think,* when the fact is that she really does care. She is just tired of "performing," putting on different masks for different people, to make them like and accept her.

Over time, Jane becomes unclear about how she really feels and who she really is. Jane starts to believe that there must be something wrong or bad about her feelings and about her. She believes that she is defective and deserves to be punished. In order to be happy, Jane represses these thoughts and feelings into her subconscious mind. When Jane represses her feelings she begins to "act out" her feelings of hurt and anger.

Lying and "acting out" are defense mechanisms that help Jane to cope as a child and teenager, but become harmful as an adult. Having this information later in life helps Jane to understand why she is "ripe for the picking" by abusers and why she remained in her abusive marriage to Dave for as long as she did.

Still, Jane is not completely healed for years to come.

***

Jane's younger son, Samuel, is still living with Jane during her time of grief, but even being with Sammy isn't enough to lift her recurring depression. Jane spends a lot of time crying and sometimes just wants to stay in bed.

Thank God for Sammy!

Jane decides to see a psychologist. She remembers what she learned from group counseling about abuse, but still needs relief from her depression. The staff at the Transition House tell her to make sure that whoever she sees is trained in domestic violence. She asks for a referral and starts seeing Dr. Mack. Jane learns that she is frozen in her grief. She stays strong for the sake of her children. She's also afraid to tell her parents for fear that they won't understand, like many of her acquaintances.

Dr. Mack helps her to find supportive friends who can understand what she is going through. Jane makes a list of people she can call on when feeling lost and depressed.

He uses music therapy, muscle testing and EMDR (eye movement desensitization reaction) that promotes the left brain and the right brain to connect with each other briefly. EMDR and other tapping methods got her thoughts to connect with her heart. Jane discovers that she has a deep rooted fear of abandonment and that she may have been sexually abused as a child.

Jane has no real memories of the latter, other than her eighth grade teacher, just fleeting pictures in her mind, a flash in time. Dr. Mack lets her know that she doesn't have to remember, but can do the therapy for this anyway. She will need supportive people in her life especially now.

Jane learns how to get over her **HABIT** of:

· **H**urt feelings

· **A**nger

· **B**itterness, and

· **I**nternal **T**ension (anxiety)

The anagram helps her to remember and to keep her on track.

According to Jill Corey and Karen McAndless-Davis, [7] the healing process from spousal abuse often has two areas: rebuilding emotions and grieving emotions. It explains the mixed feelings and roller coaster ride that women often experience. The craziness of hurtful feelings still exists alongside the desire to be with their abuser again.

Jane asks herself, *Shouldn't I be happy? Everyone else seems to think I should be. Is there something wrong with me?*

The truth is that an abusive relationship can be very traumatizing. Jane feels alone in her pain. However, she learns to be patient with herself and to allow herself to heal. As advised, she doesn't listen to her friends who try to speed up her recovery by encouraging her to "get back in the saddle." Instead, she commits to giving herself at least two years before dating again.

Jane learns and practises the "Four Stages of Codependency Recovery:"[15]

· Set up boundaries, both internal and external.

· Maintain boundaries, even in an abusive place.

· Make new healthy relationships.

· Strengthen those new bonds of friendship.

It takes her over a year to feel more in charge of her life and on the way to recovery. Jane begins to build self-esteem, gain independence, know herself better, take care of herself, and to risk new behaviors.

CHAPTER 9

RECOGNITION OF ABUSIVE BEHAVIOR AND THE CYCLE OF ABUSE

"One of the hardest things to do is to let go of what you thought was real." ~ Unknown

"The Honeymoon was wonderful but it ended too soon." ~ Jane

Have you ever been in love? Have you ever felt like you were walking on eggshells in a relationship? Has your loved one ever broken your heart so it felt like it had been ripped away? Below are the three stages of "The Honeymoon Cycle" (or "The Cycle of Abuse") from a feelings perspective:

1. The "Honeymoon" is the romantic love part

2. The "Tension" is the walking on eggshells part

3. The "Explosion" is the ripping out of your heart

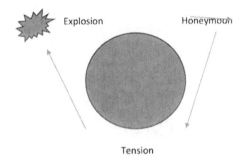

The beginning of a love relationship is the "honeymoon." This stage could last several weeks, months, or even years. In healthy relationships it may last the entire time, with a few ups and downs.

In an abusive situation, the "honeymoon" is the first stage. The abusive person treats the victim like a king or a queen. He may take her out to dinners, movies, dances, parties, and other fun activities. He'll speak sweet nothings into her ear. She'll tell everyone how wonderful he is. He will promise to give her the moon. The victim has no idea that this relationship will prove to be abusive.

In the second stage, "tension" builds. The victim feels like she is walking on eggshells, as if waiting for a volcano to erupt. The abuser is in complete control of this stage, as he is in all three stages. The victim is helpless to stop it although she earnestly wants to believe she can.

In this stage, she may hope for some control that she will never find. Healthy couples will struggle for control, but will eventually come to an acceptable balance. The victim will never get an acceptable balance. If she stays in the relationship she will eventually become unhappy, hopeless, and helpless.

The third stage is called "the explosion." The volcano erupts into belittlement, criticism, sarcasm, or an outright physical fight. This eases the tension. The cycle continues back into the honeymoon again. "Honeymoon, tension, explosion, honeymoon, tension, and explosion." In some cases, the honeymoon stage disappears and the cycle becomes "tension, explosion, tension, and explosion."

What drives this cycle is the abuser's desire for power and control over his partner. He appears to be out of control. This leaves his victim thinking it is her problem, her responsibility and her fault. Her abusive partner tells her, "You made me do it," or, "It's all your fault."

She begins to believe him. After years of abuse, it becomes part of her core belief system about herself. *If only I could change something about myself. If only I could just do things better? If only…*

The truth is, there is nothing she can do to stop the abusive cycle. Sometimes abusers may want to change, to seek help, to get better. This is the only real solution for keeping the relationship together. The victim also needs help to get over the hurt, anger, and bitterness, whether or not she stays in the relationship. The victim needs to journey to a place of forgiveness to free herself from the past. The abuser needs to make positive lasting changes to win back her trust if there can even be the slightest chance of reconciliation.

Quite often, the victim may do things that look abusive, like picking a fight just to get over the "tension" and the inevitable "explosion," with the subconscious intention of getting back to the "honeymoon stage." Nothing is black and white. The victim may be somewhat responsible but will feel like she is totally at fault for the abuse. Abusers don't feel guilty or responsible. He may pretend to act guilty and is tearful after the explosion, manipulating his way back to the honeymoon stage, but not before the explosion. He may think he is the victim (or pretend to be), but she is the real victim. There is a huge difference between the two. What a crazy life it is; the victim thinking she is the abuser and abuser thinking he is the victim, instead of the other way around.

Unfortunately, the outside world sometimes sees the female victim as the abuser too, or the cause of the problem in the relationship. She often has symptoms of depression, anxiety, or "acts out" because she doesn't know how to express her agonizing pain.

The abuser often has symptoms of one or more personality disorders, if not full-blown disorders. See "How Personality Disorders Relate to Abusive Behavior." It often takes a tragedy for people to see the real truth in domestic violence cases.

The victim may be murdered, or attacked with an attempt to kill, by the abuser. The children may be taken out of the home and put into foster care. One partner may leave in the middle of the night to escape.

The police may be called by a neighbor and one partner taken to jail. The woman and her children may be taken to a transition house for women and children who are fleeing abuse. In time, the victim may begin to heal. Learning the truth and acknowledging it is the first step towards a better life.

CHAPTER 10

MORE FACTS ABOUT DOMESTIC VIOLENCE

"Do I have a tattoo on my forehead that says abuse me?"
~ Jane

Domestic Violence is defined by international conventions and governments as "all acts of physical, sexual, psychological or economic violence that occur within the family or domestic unit or between former or current spouses or partners, whether or not the perpetrator shares or has shared the same residence with the victim. These relationships vary in duration and legal formality, and include:

- Current and former dating relationships,

- Current and former common-law relationships,

- Current and former married relationships, and

- People who are the parents of one or more children, regardless of their marital status or whether they have lived together at any time."[2]

Ninety percent of childhood sexual abuse cases occur between family members, friends and children of family members, and people known to the victim. Only 10% are carried out by complete strangers.[3] These atrocious acts, therefore, fall within the realm of domestic violence, in my opinion.

Traditional methods of upbringing, which have included spanking or humiliation, lead to the denial of suffering and humiliation, continuing into adulthood. Do you have a high pain threshold? Do you forget how you got a bruise or a cut? Maybe this was a learned response from childhood? This denial, which was essential for survival, later causes emotional blindness. This means that early denied traumas, like childhood abuse, become embedded in the brain. This keeps us from learning new information, putting it to good use, and shedding old, outdated behaviors.

What's really scary is that this retained memory of the pain and humiliations suffered, drive some people to inflict, unconsciously, the same thing onto the next generation. Or, other people from the same circumstances may become victims. Awareness is the key to change.[6]

Victims, until healed, often wonder if they have a tattoo on their forehead saying "abuse me." The truth is that they really do. These "tattoos" are not visible to the naked eye, but an abuser can spot one from miles away. Abusers seem to have x-ray vision into a victim's soul. The victim is also drawn to an abuser without knowing it. A victim does not recognize an abuser because he and she are like magnets, and abusive behavior seems normal to her; she only sees the best side of the abusive person at first. See *The Human Magnet Syndrome.*[12]

Once inside the relationship a victim may not even realize that she is being abused. If she does, she thinks it's her fault and actually feels guilty for what her abuser is doing to her. She takes on his shame and blame. The abuser knows that, and uses guilt, as part of his arsenal to control and manipulate his victim.

In the end, if she's lucky, she'll see what is happening and get out. By this time, it may be too late to reverse many of the consequences. This depends upon the victim's constitution, how long and how hurtful the abuse was.

The victim's best way to avoid serious injury is to find a safe place to stay. Leaving can be even more dangerous than staying, at least in the first few months or even years. Transition Homes have become, not only a safe haven, but a great help in a woman's recovery and in helping her to find a new life.

Many times, a woman may go back home thinking things will change and that she will get what she has always dreamed of having. The chances of that happening are one in a hundred, but the hope is so strong that it takes, on the average, seven times of leaving and returning, for the victim to leave for the final time.

Chapter 11

Tools and Guidelines to Help Identify and Prevent Abusive Relationships

Nothing in life is to be feared, it is only to be understood. Now is the time to understand more, so that we may fear less."

Red Flags – Relationship Abuse Prevention

"I wish I'd known about these red flags to warn me against abusers." ~ Jane

Watch for these signs when you are dating someone new. If the answers are "yes" to any of the following, be wary:

- Does he want to move fast in the relationship, saying "I love you," pressuring you for a commitment to get engaged, or to move in to gether?

- Has he been married, or been in a fairly long term intimate relationship before that ended badly?

- Is he extremely jealous of your friends and want to keep you for himself?

- Does he treat his own mother and father poorly?

- Does he act hurt when he doesn't get his own way or if you don't agree with his opinion. Does he threaten violence but pretend it wasn't serious?

- Did he grow up in an abusive home or was he in another abusive relationship?

- Is he abusive towards family members, using sarcasm, put-downs, or name calling?

- Does he blame others for his own misbehaviour?

- Does he have unrealistic expectations of you to meet all of his needs, and to be a perfect partner?

- Has he ever been cruel to a child or an animal?

- Does he abuse drugs or alcohol?

- Does he attempt to control what you say, wear, and/or do?

- Is he exceptionally moody going from sweet to explosive anger?

· Does he ever put you down, call you names, or curse you?

All or any of these things are warning signs of danger ahead.

Beware. Tread Carefully

Thumbnail Profile of Abusers & Victims

"Abusers and their Victims think differently and have different 'world views'." ~ Alfred Adler

Profile of an Abuser – Central, Entitled, Dominant

- Abusers goals are to have all the power and control.

- Abusers are in control of the honeymoon cycle.

- Abusers think Victims have the same goal for power and control as they do.

- Abusers are central and dominant. They believe they are entitled to be selfish.

- Abusers are irresponsible and blame others for their irresponsibility or mistakes.

- Abusers never accept the blame: "It's not my fault!"; "You made me do it."

- Abusive behavior always escalates over time, whether it's a few months, or 20 years.

- Abusers are happy and do not see a reason to change. Everything is just fine.

Profile of a Victim - Peripheral, Servant, Submissive

- Victims always take on the blame and the shame for what the abuser does to them.

- Victims are flexible and want to work things out. They want equality.

- When Victims act assertively abusers interpret the action as aggression.

- Victims are peripheral, and passive or submissive in order to keep the peace.

- Victims are responsible and take ownership of both their mistakes and their abusers.

- Victims keep hoping again and again that things will get better, but it only gets worse.

- Victims are usually scarred for life, taking a long time to heal from their wounds.

- Victims can come from all walks of life and can even be raised in a healthy home.

- Victims can be abused by anyone, including authority figures, their parents, their roommates, their children, and/or their caretakers if elderly or disabled.

QUIZ: ARE YOU A GOOD GIRL/CODEPENDENT?

(Partially based on *The Nice Girl Syndrome* by Beverly Engels)

· Can you just say "No?"

· Are you afraid to be honest because you might hurt someone's feeling?

· Do you make a habit of saying "I'm sorry?"

· Are there people in your life who take advantage of you more than once or twice?

· Are you bothered by angry people even if the anger is not directed at you specifically?

· Do you avoid confrontation at all costs?

· Are you afraid of rejection or abandonment?

· Do you believe that you need to be protected?

· Do you stand up for people who you think are misunderstood or misjudged?

· Do you believe you don't have a right to criticize a job poorly done if you didn't volunteer to do it yourself?

· Are you attracted to bad boys, or girls?

· Are you always fair to others even when they are unfair to you?

- Are you afraid to ask your boss for a raise or to work for a higher salary?

- Do you usually put others before yourself?

- Do you allow yourself to be unhealthy or unkempt?

- Are you sometimes depressed?

If you answered yes to two or more of these questions, you have some Good Girl in you. "Being nice" is too high of a price to pay in today's world.

TYPES OF ABUSERS

"Abusiveness is like poison ivy. You have to pull it out by the roots. A man's core attitudes and beliefs must change." ~ Lundy Bancroft

Bancroft, author of *Why Does He Do That?* [9] describes many types of abusers. Here are just three examples:

One type of abuser believes that he is above criticism and thinks he is a very loving and giving spouse. If his victim is unhappy about anything it's always her fault, even if he drops his responsibilities. His partner should not place any demands on him but be grateful for whatever he chooses to give. He is a disordered individual who cannot face the reality of his actions. He therefore invents a new reality as a defense mechanism.

Another type thinks his victim is crazy. She gets upset excessively. He thinks he can convince others that she is the one who needs help. He can remain calm because he believes he's not abusive, even when very cruel. He knows exactly what to do or say to upset her. This is "blame shifting." *I'm not crazy; she's the one with the mental health problem.*

Still another needs to control her every move to make sure his victim does everything his way and has no one else or nothing else in her life besides him. Only he knows the right way to do things. He is going to keep her in her lowly place. He says he loves her more than anything or anyone, but she disgusts him. He can't deal with his own nasty behavior. Instead he uses "projection" and tells himself, *I'm not disgusting. She is.*

These types of abusers use defense mechanisms to avoid facing their own bad behavior. "Projection" and "blame shifting" are the most common. They mainly cross internal boundaries. Besides *Why Does He Do That,* I recommend reading, *The Emotionally Abused Woman*, Beverly Engel. She describes different types of victims and abusers and the worst combinations of the two.[10]

CHAPTER 12

HOW PERSONALITY DISORDERS RELATE TO ABUSIVE BEHAVIOR

"…Darkness cannot drive out darkness; only light can do that. Hate cannot drive out hate; only love can do that."

~ Martin Luther King, Jr.

Many abusers have a Personality Disorder (PD), more than one, or some of the symptoms of a PD. They were most likely abused and perhaps even hated as children. Their lives were lacking in love and attention either because they lacked the intuition and intelligence to please their parental abusers; they experienced extreme abuse; they were smothered with overprotective parents, or they were sexually abused.

Antisocial, Narcissistic, & Borderline PDs are the most dangerous, and most likely to overlap one another. Their victims are extremely codependent according to Rosenberg's Self-Theory. Many people have a mild narcissistic nature and can have healthy relationships with mild codependents. Personality Disorders are intense and must be diagnosed by professionals.

Four disorders that are most relevant for domestic violence are the "Cluster B" Personality Disorders.[8]

Antisocial Personality Disorder

Sociopaths and Psychopaths fall into the category of Antisocial Personality Disorder. They are currently considered interchangeable terms in psychology. People with this disorder are unable to put themselves into someone else's shoes, unless they want to for their own selfish reasons. This is why they can seem so pleasant, and can then turn into a monster only moments later. They are liars, criminals (if caught,) aggressive, impulsive and irresponsible people having no remorse. Sociopaths think that it's okay to take whatever they want and to commit crimes, even heinous crimes, as long as they don't get caught.

To avoid being manipulated by these dangerous people, try to recognize their following "modus operandi." First, they assess a victims' weaknesses, defenses and possible use. Second, they try to impress whoever is in charge, like parents, or bosses of corporations. They manipulate people's ability to gain resources for themselves, like money. Once they have received what they want, they abandon ship.[11]

If they don't get what they want they will retaliate, even to the point of torture and/or murder.

Narcissistic Personality Disorder

Narcissism can range from mild to severe. Mild Narcissists make good actors, musicians and in other careers where they need confidence. Those who are diagnosed with Narcissistic Personality Disorder (NPD) are obsessed with the need to feel understood, to be the center of attention, to be superior, and to take advantage of others using manipulation, threats, or whatever works. They lack empathy and think that they deserve to be treated better than others. They have a sense of entitlement. They are "emotional vampires," soaking up attention and praise like a sponge, always craving more. NPDs can become enraged if they don't get enough attention or are criticized. They can even commit criminal offenses when this happens, just like sociopaths.

Borderline Personality Disorder

The same is true for individuals with Borderline Personality Disorder, commonly called BPD. They can sometimes be as violent as sociopaths and to have narcissistic rages. BPDs have a poor self-image and problems in relationships with others. They have rapid mood swings from irritability to depression, and experience projection, paranoia, and/or a lack of empathy. They often self-medicate with alcohol and/or drugs, never experiencing the highs like Bipolar individuals do. They often engage in binge eating, promiscuity, cutting, or putting themselves in harm's way, such as attempted suicide. All three personality disorders above are at high risk to manipulate and abuse their partners and others.

Histrionic Personality Disorder

Individuals with Histrionic Personality Disorder have some of the symptoms of Narcissism and BPD but are much less likely to be violent abusers. Their distinguishing characteristic is that of a "Drama Queen." They crave attention, but tend to use words rather than violence to express their anger.

Bipolar Disorder

Bipolar Disorder is NOT a Personality Disorder. People with Bipolar Disorder (also known as Manic Depression), have some symptoms similar to BPD and can be misdiagnosed. For example, promiscuity and self-medication can be common to both. Symptoms of Bipolar Disorder are extreme highs and lows that are caused by brain chemistry more than life circumstances. They often make poor decisions by trying to make sense of their feelings, assigning it to a life circumstance. Bipolar Disorder I and Bipolar II disorders both have about 50% genetic and 50% thought pattern abnormalities.

Only in Bipolar 1 Disorder and in BPD are there psychotic episodes. In the stage of a psychotic high or depression it is possible that someone with Bipolar Disorder can cause harm to themselves or others. The reason however, is not projection, paranoia, and/or a lack of empathy, like it can be in Borderline Personality Disorder. Rather someone with Bipolar 1 Disorder has lost touch with reality and may fear the invasion of robots or something totally unrealistic.

People with Bipolar Disorder are almost always the victims.

GLOSSARY OF TERMS

Acting-Out – an individual who is unable to feel or to understand their own feelings. They literally act-out their feelings in wild, inappropriate behaviors which can lead to: promiscuity, fighting, pornography, gambling or drugs. They "act out" their repressed feelings.

Blame Shifting – a type of defense mechanism similar to projection. Instead of taking on the blame and shame of their own behavior, they shift it to another. They may or may not do this intentionally.

Boundaries – can be internal and/or external acceptable limits expected by an individual for others to respect and honor. Narcissists and abusers walk all over other people's boundaries if they can. Codependents and victims have few or no boundaries. They need to learn to create them from the inside out. It starts with building back self-esteem, self-control, self-respect, and courage.

Cluster B Personality Disorders (PDs) or Tendencies – Histrionic, Narcissism, Borderline, and Antisocial PDs range from mild to severe. Narcissistic tendencies are in all of the "Cluster B" PDs and even in some fairly normal people.

Mid- range tendencies or diagnosed personality disorders in this group are related to abusive behavior.

Codependent – an individual with a psychological condition (not recognized as a mental illness in the DSM IV), which shows up in relationships. Codependents give more love, respect, and care for another than they receive, expect, or even dare to request. With severe codependency, anger, bitterness and resentment build up inside. Whether or not they leave a relationship they are likely to repeat the same pattern with another partner who is very narcissistic or abusive.

Complicated Grief – lasts longer than normal grief. It is an emotional rollercoaster ride. It's worse than if a loved one had died of normal causes. The griever has to deal with, not only the loss, but also the belief that she was the cause of the breakup, especially if she was the one who left.

Defense Mechanisms – unhealthy ways of behaving, and thinking to protect oneself in crisis situations. They can become habits and difficult to overcome. Projection, blame shifting, lying, people-pleasing, detachment, and acting-out all fall into this category.

Depression – can be normal sadness/grief. It can also be related to a change of hormones during the menstrual period, post-partum, or menopause (including pre-, current and post-.) Clinical depression is a mood disorder caused by a chemical imbalance in the brain.

Detachment – can occur either when an individual is doing something that goes against her values or is suffering more pain than can be handled. The individual feels like she isn't in her own body, but is observing her actions from a distance.

Emotional Vampires – People who soak up attention and praise like a sponge. They are always craving more and will soak you dry if you let them.

Grooming – Preparing someone to act in a particular way so they can be taken advantage of. The predator does this prior to childhood sexual abuse or in abusive intimate partnerships.

Red Flags – Warning signs that could indicate abusiveness. Look for these signs in a potential partner.

Paranoia – Unfounded belief that individuals, social service agencies or other things are watching and out to get them.

People Pleasing – trying to be all things to all people; putting on different masks; denial of self to gain esteem, safety and love. When someone is a people pleaser it's impossible to be authentic and assertive.

Projection – total denial of our own bad behaviors like anger, dishonesty, manipulation, and abusiveness. We cannot face them, thus see incorrectly the same behavior in another person.

Sarcasm – passive aggressive, hurtful, witty jokes that cover up the truth.

Self-Theory – The magnetic attraction between two intimate partners of equal narcissistic and codependent polarities. Dr. Rosenberg, in *The Human Magnet Syndrome*, devised a scale from one to five, five being the most severe. Narcissists can range from a positive one to a positive five, while codependents can range from negative one to a negative five. Couples rating one or two (one positive and one negative) are healthy, while ratings of four and five are dysfunctional or unhealthy. The number threes are in the middle.

Subconscious Mind - memories that are below one's level of consciousness, happenings from birth to the age of five or six. When we were helpless, we were unable to make the decision whether or not to accept certain values and beliefs. The subconscious mind also retains memories of pain and humiliations suffered. Intolerable memories and feelings are "repressed."

Suggested Reading & Resources

· *Darkness to Light's Stewards of Children Interactive Workbook Your Personal Prevention Plan* http://www.D2L.org

The following books are available at: http://www.amazon.com

· *The Courage to Heal – A Guide for Women Survivors of Child Sexual Abuse* by Ellen Bass and Laura Davis

· *The Courage to Heal Workbook – for Women and Men Survivors of Child Sexual Abuse* by Laura Davis

- *The Emotionally Abused Woman* by Beverly Engel, and other books by the same author.

- *The Human Magnet Syndrome – Why We Love People Who Hurt Us – Emotional Manipulators, Codependents & Dysfunctional Relationships* by Ross Rosenberg, M.Ed., LCPC, CADC

- *Love is a Choice Workbook – Recovery for Codependent Relationships* by Robert Hemfelt and Frank Minirth, and other similar books.

- *Why Does He Do That? – Inside the Minds of Angry and Controlling Men* by Lundy Bancroft, and other books by the same author.

- *When Love Hurts – A Woman's Guide to Understanding Abuse in Relationships* by Jill Corey and Karen McAndless-Davis

Other Resources and Search Terms for Google:

Transition Homes and Shelters Counseling Services Crisis Lines

WORLD WIDE WEBSITES

S.A.F.E (Stop Abuse for Everyone): http://www.safe4all.org http://domesticviolencestatistics.org/domestic-violence -statistics/

http://www.statisticbrain.com/domestic-violence-abuse -stats/

www.clarkprosecutor.org/html/domviol/facts.htm

http://www.unwomen.org/en/what-we-do/ending-violence-against-women/facts-and-figures

http://www.stopvaw.org/prevalence_of_domestic_violence

https://www.youtube.com/ How to know if you are dating a Psychopath

http://humanmagnetsyndrome.com/

Videos on The Human Magnet Syndrome, Narcissism, and Codependency

Canadian (BC *) Resources

http://www.pssg.gov.bc.ca/victimservices/help/counselling.htm#children *

http://www2.gov.bc.ca *

http://www.canadianwomen.org

Public Health Canada: http://www.phac-aspc.gc.ca/ncfv-cnivf/maleabus-eng.php

includes a pdf list of the following:

- Police Service - Family, Youth and Violent Crime Section

- RCMP - Victim Services

- Provincial Government -Provincial Mental Health Boards

- The YMCA, some centers have a Family Violence Prevention Program

- Community and Social Service offices

- Mental Health-Crisis Helpline (24 hour) 1-800-584-3578

In violent or life and death situations, or crimes in progress call 9-1-1.

ST. JOHN THE BAPTIST PARISH LIBRARY
2920 NEW HIGHWAY 51
LAPLACE, LOUISIANA 70068

ABOUT THE AUTHOR

 Beverly Wallin grew up in Calgary, Alberta, Canada and has travelled all over Canada, U.S.A., Mexico, Costa Rica and the Caribbean.

She has the equivalent of a Master's degree in Psychology from the University of Western Ontario, a Master's degree in Counseling Psychology from the Adler School, Chicago, as well as a Coaching diploma from Health Coaching University, Florida.

Wallin has worked with seniors, and individuals of all ages with mental disabilities, Most importantly she has counseled victims of domestic violence for over 20 years.

Beverly knows firsthand the damage that abuse can cause, how to avoid it and how to heal from it.

Beverly now wants to reach out to the world with her knowledge and experience in the hopes of putting a stop to abuse against men, women and children.

Beverly Wallin

Beverly started her writing career in the northern city of Whitehorse, Yukon, Canada with a column in the Whitehorse Star Newspaper. She has written many e-zine articles online and has published *You Don't have to be a Wimp to be Abused – An Easy Guide to Understanding Domestic Violence against Men.* She now lives on Canada's West Coast, in White Rock, BC, right beside the ocean's beaches.

Beverly also loves to paint using oil and acrylics, and to write poetry.

Wallin plans to publish a book of poetry with copies of her paintings. a novel, some novellas, and more self-help books about domestic violence.

Message from the Author

This book is about domestic violence against women. Jane is a fictional character, based on a composite of true stories. All names and places have been changed to protect those individuals. It helps to show how it would feel to be in the shoes of a victim. Although it is told in story form for a large part of the book, it is full of factual information on the prevalence, types, and whys of abuse, plus warnings on how to avoid and recognize abuse. It contains lots of resources:

· reading for those who want to learn more about the subject

· where a victim can get help, and

· how they can help themselves.

If you have learned something valuable in reading this book, and know someone who could benefit from reading it too, please consider doing one of the following things:

· Gift them a copy of this book

· Write a positive review on amazon.com so others in need can find and benefit from this important message.

·   Help women at <u>www.womenthrive.org/DVAM</u> 1

As I have noted from the start, abuse can happen to anyone, and bringing consciousness to this subject is critical. If you know of a man in an abusive situation you can direct them to my parallel book for men, which chronicles another fictional character, Fred, based on a composite of true stories.

You can also learn more at my websites:

<u>http://www.coachingforhealthandwellness.com</u>

<u>http://bevwallin.com</u>

<u>http://amazon.com/author/beverlywallin</u>

Email <u>bevwallin@gmail.com</u> to get on my list and be informed when new books come out.

Available on Amazon and Amazon kindle since 2014.

ENDNOTES

1. www.womenthrive.org/DVAM

2. http://en.wikipedia.org/wiki/Domestic_violence

3. *Darkness to Light's Stewards of Children Interactive Workbook – Your Personal Prevention Plan* www.D2L.org

4. *The Nice Girl Syndrome: Stop Being Manipulated and Abused -- and Start Standing Up for Yourself* by Beverly Engel

5. *The Truth Will Set You Free – Overcoming Emotional Blindness and Finding Your True Self* by Alice Miller and Andrew Jenkins

6. *Lovefraud–*www.lovefraud.com/2009/01/08/emotional-blindness-and-the-sociopath/ by Pearl … Also on You Tube

7. *When Love Hurts* by Jill Corey and Karen McAndless-Davis

8. *Cluster B Personality Disorders* by Kristalyn Salters-Peneault, PhD. http://bpd.about.com/od/relatedconditions/a/clusterB.htm

9. *Why Does He Do That: Inside the Minds of Angry and Controlling Men* by Lundy Bancroft

10. *The Emotionally Abused Woman – Overcoming Destructive Patterns and Reclaiming Yourself* - by Beverly Engel

11. *Snakes in Suits – When Psychopaths Go to Work* by Paul Babiak, Ph.D and Robert D. Hare, Ph.D.

12. *The Human Magnet Syndrome – Why We Love People Who Hurt Us – Emotional Manipulators Codependents & Dysfunctional Relationships* by Ross Rosenburg, M.Ed., LCPC, CADC

13. *The Cinderella Complex – Women's Hidden Fear of Independence* by Colette Dowling

14. <u>http://humanmagnetsyndrome.com/</u> and other You Tube Vide

CPSIA information can be obtained
at www.ICGtesting.com
Printed in the USA
LVOW08s0039091116
512211LV00007B/165/P